There Is A MESSAGE IN MY WORDS

WRITTEN BY

DONALD DAVID ROBINSON THE II

Table of contents:

1. 15 cell
2. A future
3. A message to my brothers
4. At night I cry
5. Be yourself
6. Being a man
7. Being the best man I can be
8. Black people
9. Caught in the crossfire
10. Chase my enemies away
11. Covered in darkness
12. Dear God
13. Dedicated to my Grandparents
14. Dedicated to my wife
15. Died to get rich
16. Don't lose hope
17. Dying in my own blood
18. Forgiveness, friendship and love
19. My real friends
20. Get your education
21. God is on our side
22. Hard to walk away
23. He struggles
24. Heaven is my finish line
25. Hey it's ok to do the right thing
26. I ask God
27. I need music
28. I pray
29. I understand
30. I'm gonna to let it shine
31. In memory of my friend Stephen Sudden

32. In memory of RayShawn
33. Life or death which do you choose
34. Lights flashing
35. Mothers love
36. My beautiful black brothers and sisters
37. My thoughts of the world today
38. On a negative path
39. Peace
40. Secrets hidden within his heart
41. So you want to be tough
42. Stop being a THOT
43. Stop the gang war
44. The realest words I ever wrote
45. To my brothers
46. To my father
47. My siblings
48. To whom it may concern
49. Together you and I are stronger
50. Truly my lady
51. Untitled
52. Violence is it worth it
53. We live in insane times
54. We need to communicate
55. Welcome to Harris Ave also known as H Block
56. Whatever it takes
57. What help do we get in here
58. When I look into your eyes
59. Who am I
60. Willing to learn
61. You are my everything
62. You are my strength
63. Victoria Nina Simone A poem for my daughter
64. Simone

15 Cell:

Another night gone

Time seems so long

As the gates close

I'm doing all I can to remain strong

Tears drop from my eyes

Feeling like I am in the pit of hell

Lights out welcome to 15 cell.

In here I'm no boy in their eyes this man is just a convict

Another criminal wearing an orange jump suit looking like a pumpkin on Halloween

This environment is not a good one at all but I believe god will pull me through.

Selling drugs living a foul life playing the dirty game

I can't be mad at no one but myself because I chose to do wrong so I accept full blame

Now I am doing time in Nassau County Correctional Facility

Temporarily I've lost all my rights trying to avoid unnecessary fights

Doing hundreds of push-ups to get through the sleepless nights.

Surrounded by men of all kind

In this place at times it's hard to find a piece of mind

I got to watch who I talk to watch what I say because blood is the price to pay

So from bad company I choose to stay away.

Oh shit the turtles are coming in got to get rid of my merchandise

And the home made wine soaking in the cup watching out for the rat in the next cell

Because I know his bitch ass might tell it's a shakedown I hear the C.O. say crack 15 cell.

A FUTURE

Day after day I am watching so many teenagers lose their lives or freedom

to violence.

Both male and female running away from home,

Disrespecting their parents or the ones

Who care for them because they father be in the streets.

Young girls thinking it's cool to lose their virginity at the age of 15

To 5 or more guys believing its ok to be a whore.

Young boys fronting like they are above the law

Until they end up taking that bus ride up north

Because they wasn't strong enough to walk away from the nonsense;

Too gangster to swallow their pride.

Last night I watched a father cry because his child was shot twice in the head,

Bullets sprung out hit the wrong house. The little girl was sleeping in her bed.

It's so sad to see that eight year old boy ask his mom,

"Just like Dad, will I go to prison at 16? Come home at 20, and end up dead?"

Pay attention to the words that I speak because we are living in wicked times,

We must get it together, be positive role models for our youth

And give them what we stole from ourselves.

A FUTURE.

A message to my brothers:

Just like you, my choice of a weapon was either my hands or anything that could bring you serious bodily harm such as a gun or a knife there was a time that I was not afraid to use either one.

Just like you I sat in a jail cell only to realize that I am becoming a monster drowning in my own misery searching for happiness and a better way to live.

Brother I am here to tell you that change is beautiful especially when you are applying goodness to your life and never be afraid to pray regardless your mood pray trust me God hears you and he will answer you maybe not when you feel he should but he will answer you.

If you were bad enough to sin be strong enough to pray calling on God is the best call anyone can every make the call is free and you can talk to him as long as you choose I know it is not easy out here in this big world that can at times seem cold and vicious but you can make it through you are strong and you will survive.

There are times when I want to hurt people really bad stop them from breathing but I give thought to what I will lose and who I will lose and falling victim to their nonsense just is not worth losing what I have fought hard to build up and prayed for day in and day out no my brother it's not worth it.

I teach myself to walk away from trouble because I know it is the right thing to do and plus it saves me a lot of trouble and money because no a day's people like to slap lawsuits on you for any reason they can find.

Listen life will be challenging at times but as I mentioned just pray turn to God and ask him to guide your footsteps the right way and just to let you know a book that is resourceful and reliable it is called the Bible.

AT NIGHT I CRY

I dream a dream,

I hide my pain with a fake smile,

No one knows I'm hurting except God,

I try to do many things to keep my mind off of the struggle I'm going through,

But nothing seems to work,

Like a bird, away I want to fly,

Because at night I cry.

How could I let this happen?

Why was I so naïve to walk right into the devil's trap?

I was blinded by things I thought was good,

But really it was wicked,

Every night on my knees I ask God,

Why? So

At night I cry.

Filled with shame and gloom,

I close my eyes, wishing I was home,

In my room,

But when I open my eyes I'm still in this 6x9 cell,

Feeling like I'm not too far from hell,

This is my punishment,

For all the hurt I caused and every lie I told,

Yes, for all the hurt and every lie, At night I cry.

Be Yourself

Don't follow those who have no direction,

And if you cannot find your own way,

Which is positive?

Ask God to lead the way,

As long as you hold his hand.

Drugs and alcohol will only stop you from succeeding,

Those who are disrespectful and live to start trouble will die a horrible death,

Never converse or journey with fools,

Because they do not know what they are talking about,

Or where they are going.

When you hide from reality,

You blind yourself from the truth,

Instead of being a fool,

Be yourself no matter what challenges comes your way.

Being a Man

He knows nothing about being a man, blindsided by negativity of the streets. He has no clue of what a man is or what he stands for.

In his mind it's all about how much money he can make by being the neighborhood narcotic supplier or how many women he can get bragging about how much time in jail he spent. Smoking weed, disrespecting his family, party after party unable to see reality.

Even I admit I am far from perfect, but I have to give effort to live right, strive hard to be a better man than I was yesterday. So I start off by getting on my knees to pray because only God can transform me into the real man I need to be.

I had to learn that a man doesn't walk around with his pants hanging off his ass, or talking words that don't make any sense. Every time the boys in blue came through I'm jumping fences, hiding the pistol and crack underneath abandoned cars. Get locked up, forced to be a soldier behind bars.

I respect the man who has his own business or holding down a 9-5, taking care of his family as well as himself; living right never walking around broke blaming others for his problems, purposely looking for someone to fight or drowning his sorrows in drugs and booze.

Being The Best Man I Can Be:

I am far from perfect but I must give effort to be the best man I possibly can be.

As I grow and mature and learn from past poor choices and mistakes I realize more and more of what a man must do, how a man must be let me explain a bit deeper.

If I see myself as a man I must do manly things and not carry myself as a teenage boy, I want my brothers to understand something's I pray my words encourage as many men as possible.

Leaving the streets alone and turning away from negative people was the best choice that I could ever make my life is so much more peaceful.

To stop hanging out at bars and spending unnecessary money fronting like I got it like that when I really don't is definitely another good thing I have done as well.

To give effort to control my anger and not let small things get the best of me has helped me overcome many obstacles in my life. So that when the real serious things occur I am smart enough and humble enough to make wise decisions.

To realize that my black brothers are out here struggling makes me want to help my brothers as much as I can the more I elevate in life and the more I learn it's only right I lend a helping hand to my brothers in need.

To be the best husband to my wife father to my daughter son to my mother brother to my siblings is what I look forward to doing and also being there for my aunts uncles cousins and friends in a positive manner is very important to me.

To be able to come home and receive the love from my wife and daughter when the job and the outside world appears to be so cold in cruel is the greatest feeling I can receive and to have a beautiful God fearing woman in my life who understands that it's not easy for a black man out here at times is truly a blessing.

As a black man I enjoy working hard for my family making sure that the bills are paid food is in the refrigerator clothes are on our backs and heat is in the house is all that matters to me.

To be able to provide a happy life to my family such as going on vacations and giving them gifts or saying a word to them that will make them smile and encourage them to do well in life is important to me in many ways.

To stay out of jail and unnecessary trouble is what I focus on because honestly going to jail getting into trouble living a disrespectful life is just not cool.

To make a mends with anyone I have hurt or offended in any kind of way is a thing I must do because I don't want to leave this earth knowing that I still had people mad or hating me for something I did or said.

To build a solid foundation for my wife and daughter I take pride in and to educate my daughter about being respectful, successful and establishing her own is what I fight hard to do because I am raising her not to depend on no man and not to deal with any man who is only out for one thing or to use and abuse her.

I look back on my past and there are something's I wish I never did but then again I feel those things had to happen in order for me to mature as a man and become a good man.

As a man I ask God to stay in my life keep me strong and never let me stray in any kind of way I ask God to please take away all that's bad inside of me and replace with the good things that should be in me.

As a strong black man let me always stay loyal to my wife and treat her as God has instructed me to and always keep my mind and heart on my own wife rather to let my eyes wonder upon another woman.

It's not easy but as a man I must give the effort every day in order to be a great man never losing focus of what is important. Brothers once a black man figures out what's really important in life with Gods assistance the black man will become better and stronger in every area of his life.

It really is alright to be a grown man and to be responsible I will never be afraid to be obligated to take of my business professionally and personally as a man.

Brothers trust and believe if we learn to stop letting nonsense interfere with our lives we will be able to enjoy the most beautiful life.

I hope these words I speak encourage my brothers and all men all over the land I will continue to pray for my brothers and ask God to take away your pain hurt and anger and replace it with joy and peace and if no one has told you my brothers I want you to know you are loved, loved by me and our heavenly father its ok for black men to love and respect each other respect and compassion for one another would really make a difference in our homes and our communities I pray it be amongst us all.

Being a man also means that I must never put my family, friends or myself in harm's way of any sort I must watch my drinking and not caught up with drugs and things that will destroy my mind and body.

Black People:

Let's stop killing and hurting one another

Instead let us respect and love one another

But first we must learn to love and respect our selves

Stop making the prison system rich by spending your time

Behind bars, stop making us look like animals because we are not animals

We are beautiful black people do you understand we are beautiful.

We are being killed and attacked by law enforcement

We are being killed and attacked by other cultures

And on a daily basis we are killing and attacking each other

This does not make any sense.

Why do we embarrass ourselves on T.V. selling our souls for a bit of fame?

Why do our beautiful black women feel they have to be naked and refer?

To themselves as bitches like it's cool or jumping around sleeping with random men bragging about how they slept with another woman's husband or boyfriend "Really" Goddammit black woman respect yourself.

Why does the black man think it's cool to walk around showing his ass man pull your

Damn pants up, what real black man labels himself a nigger

What real black man puts him behind bars due to committing crime?

And please tell me what real black man goes around disrespecting women

And real black man neglects his family, I mean come on black people let's get it together

We are strong we are beautiful we are amazing use your God given talent for good

Not bad we must stop destroying ourselves and each other for far too long

We have been in the pit of hell let us break the chains of violence, drugs, disease, abuse and other wicked things that appear to hold us back let us stop being jealous of one another acting

Like crabs in a barrel instead of being uneducated let's get educated

Get enlightened and stand for a positive purpose rather to fall victim

To a life of sin please black people learn your worth know that you are God's child

And he loves you and wants you to be amazing never let no one devalue you because black people you are truly a blessing.

Caught In The Cross Fire:

A young man's dreams have been destroyed,

So intelligent and precious to many,

His life meant nothing to the ones who were shooting off the guns.

Can we stop the Violence?

His mother's tears run heavy like a water fall

As the detectives leave her house the neighbors can

Here her scream out in pain saying no not my child not my baby

My heart can feel her agony a mother who is devoted to her family

She now has to burry a child because of some foolishness I wonder if

The shooter knew that this young man had dreams of becoming a

Doctor now that dream will never be lived out I brings

A nasty feeling to my stomach to see how bad the world is really getting

And how some of the young people have no respect nor regard for

Human life.

He just wanted to have fun like every other person does he was only going to stay

At the party for 2 hours just to speak to some friends and then suddenly a fight

Broke out guns were pulled and then let off and as he tried to run for cover he was shot in the back.

This kind of violence is growing stronger every day while we are losing

So many people both male and female we must stop the madness stop using guns

And violence to solve your issues there is a better way to resolve conflict

It should not take for a person to end up dead or in prison to realize that

Violence is not the answer all lives matter and so now this mother

Must notify family and friends and make funeral arrangements

When she should really be getting family together for her son's graduation

So many mothers have had to experience this horror but we can make it stop

If we come together and be peaceful and when we do have an issue let us

Not resort to violence Damn shame another life lost due to being caught in the

Cross fire.

Chase my enemies away

Lord these drug dealers are trying to tempt me to get back in the game but I cannot be distracted by the distracted no never.

So I get down on my knees and pray to you father for your unconditional love, guidance and protection to stay away from my enemies because no real friend would try to tempt me to do wrong.

Fake people amongst me but I got my eye on them all

I am doing good living a clean healthy life but I see they are praying for my downfall but what they don't know is God is my protector and I am going to be alright as long as I stay with God.

I know longer live a life of lying, cheating, stealing and hurting others no longer do I sell drugs to people just to make a dollar I get up every day work hard for mines as a man is supposed to and it feels damn good to be a man.

I put my faith and trust in you Lord, bless me with the power and courage to transgress no more, lord I will never play with you like a game because you are not to be played with or disrespected I just ask you to please chase my enemies away and keep me safe yes please

Chase my enemies away.

Covered In Darkness:

Covered in darkness, crying out for help, searching for a way out of this misery, my body feeling half dead full of pain blinded by the devils madness, I never saw it coming.

This pain is too much for me to bare I see the end coming oh yes it's truly near I don't think I can hold on I been fighting for far too long.

My mind is weak how I used to be so strong what's wrong with me I can't lose this fight I refuse to give up but it is as if I have no energy left in me then suddenly from a far I hear this voice speaking to me but no one is in the room I look up and the chills that run through my body tell me that it is you God and I am listening.

God told me I will refresh you and tomorrow you will continue your fight because I am your protector and where I have ordered your steps no one can stop I knew right then and there that God was truly with me.

God continued to say to me as you travel the road I have instructed you to walk down I want you to encourage others to follow my ways and you also must make peace with anyone you have wronged and if they wronged you, you do as I say and forgive them but you must forgive them from your heart no other reason just forgive them because I have forgiven you.

God told me that he allowed me to go through the storm so that I can realize what I was doing was wrong and that he knows my heart and he forgives me the love of God is unexplainable but all so wonderful this is why I choose to walk with God because he forgave me for so many things and saved me from death many times stopped me from becoming a drug dealer, drug addict and an alcoholic I am just an imperfect man doing my best to follow the way of God I don't always do as I am supposed to but still I trust and believe in God and I ask him for strength every day that he opens my eyes.

Life is so beautiful when you are living it with God.

Dear God:

Hear broken once again. Why did I give him the gun? It should be me sitting in that cell. God, please save my brother, take him out of the pit of hell;

Father, have mercy on my brother. Please forgive him, I beg you to help him. He deserves to live life right. Can you teach him? Father, please teach him how to be a man;

I lay here choking on my tears because his problem is half my fault. It should be me getting arraigned, not my brother. Forgive me, Father, I've sinned again. Please, don't let me lose my very best friend;

I know he was in the wrong but please have mercy, have mercy on his soul. Renew his spirit, clean him thoroughly. Jehovah, teach him your ways so that he can walk right;

Please don't let my brother do heavy time. I know he has to give them some, but please not too much. He needs your help, Father; touch his heart, mind, and spirit. Your power let him fear it. Let us all fear it so that we will live right and follow your laws always and forever.

Love your son,

Pop

P/S: Jehovah, please hear me cry out to you. My brother needs your help. Free us all from the power of sin.

Dedicated to my Grandparents Ernest and Gertrude Butts:

Thoughts of you never leave my mind oh how I wish you were still here what I wouldn't do to see both of your faces again.

Grandpa you left me with so many memories so many times I laugh to myself about things you would do and say. Although you had your struggles like every other man you were a good man and I love you for all the good things you did for your family I love you for always letting my bad butt stay with you ride around with you even though I would tell Grandma on you, you still let me be with you. I am thankful for the butt whippings because somewhere down the line they saved my life and kept me from repeating the same poor choice twice.

I know you watch over the family every day I just feel it and believe it deep in my heart you truly are still here with us.

Grandma what I wouldn't do to give you hug and tell you I love you just one more time you were the greatest Grandmother ever you always made sure the family was good and we had everything we needed oh how you spoiled us I never had a chance to really say I am sorry for the bad things I did when you were alive so I want you to know I sincerely apologize I also want to thank you for giving me my first children's bible and teaching me about God and instilling positive family values in me trust me it has helped me as I get older.

The family misses you so much I am sure you and Grandpa are up in heaven hand in hand loving one another just as God intended you too you and Grandpa are the sun that shine downs up us and you are the 2 brightest stars in the sky during the night that I look to when I need to feel your love and talk to you.

The family goes through trials and tribulations but you would be proud of us all your children are well, and your Grandchildren are doing well. Your Great Grandchildren are so beautiful you would spoil them rotten as you did us, how I want to see you again I pray God sends you back to us oh how great that would be I would hold you both in my arms forever and never let you go. I would tell you everything that has happened in my life the good and the bad.

I wish we could eat dinner together and you were here to enjoy all the family gatherings enjoying life with the family, please just know that we love you both and we miss you and we look for the day to be with you again.

Dedicated to My Wife:

You're the air that I breathe the love that I need, want and deserve and I love you for being you.

There were times I sure you wanted to give up and file for divorce and I know when it got to you like that how you would pray and let God be the guiding force and put us back to where you and I needed to be.

13 years strong and you are that same beautiful young lady I met back then I am still in love with your smile warm touch and delicious kisses.

We continue to aggravate one another but you know what we are together to do so and later on laugh about it enjoying life with you and our daughter is all I want to continue to do, you and Victoria are my joy and always I will love you both.

The only thing I ask of you my wife is don't ever give up on me and I pray you never let satin into our family and your loyalty is important to me to trust you with it all is all I ask of you keep smiling for me because your smile gives me life and encourages me to work hard for you and our daughter and remember I will always love you through the highs and lows the thunder and rain and the sunshine you will forever be my love.

Died to Get Rich:

How much longer will it take for my brothers and sisters?

To realize that there is nothing good in the streets,

Disease, Jail, and Death are the only prizes?

My heart aches because month after month, year after year I attend many funerals.

As I write these words I reminisce about my friend,

Whose life came to an end at an early age?

Chasing all that was unreal, playing the wrong game, slinging crack-cocaine.

It didn't take him long to become the man…

You know that class a type of dude; money,

Houses, cars, clothes, jewels for days…

The most feared who rolled with an unstoppable team,

Popping bottles like your favorite rapper or movie star

But that path he walked did not lead very far.

I can remember it like yesterday as we stepped out of the bar.

It was like I was the only one who seen the black masks and machine guns;

The bullets started flying; bodies were dropping to the ground leaking heavy, slowly dying.

How I didn't get hit only god knows, because he is the one who saved me.

Today I still ask why my friend? Why wasn't he spared?

15 bullets ripped through his flesh one by one how could he escape death?

Tears dripped down from his eyes… he held my hand; said,

"Father forgives us" took his last breath and went home.

I think back to when my friend was looking to become

A doctor, lawyer, maybe even a big time movie producer…

It's ill how no doctor could save him because if he would have lived he was facing five different cases for the feds. So not even the best lawyer could get him off

The only thing that could happen is that a documentary be done on his life.

How RICH it would make the producer.

How my man died was fowl, yes indeed,

But I know that how he lived Death came with the territory.

So readers, please pay attention to the words I write.

I pray my people wake up and see the light.

I look at how my friend was taken over by

Drugs, money, women, and material things that had no real value.

What did he get out of it? Nothing at all except a Casket

My friend dug himself into a ditch and died just to get rich.

Don't lose hope:

Ladies when your man leaves you and your child I know it's not an easy thing to always handle especially when there is so much responsibility involved but just remember God is good all the time and he will make sure that you and your child will be alright just put your trust in him and you will see a beautiful thing happen.

Ladies be inspired to always be good women be good to yourselves and your child or children because children need good mothers and I know it's not fair you have to pick up the slack but you have to just pull up your big girl pants tighten your belt and keep pushing on.

Just because your child's father did not appreciate you trust and believe there's a man out there waiting for you wanting to love you and only you so please don't give up on life or let what your child's father did break you down you are beautiful and intelligent you are a shining star.

I am talking to all the woman all over the world because you need and deserve to be encouraged when you are going through the struggles of life just know that you are not alone and also know that I care even if you never met me trust and believe I care for you at all times.

Ladies you are to respected and treated like queens but you must first respect and treat yourselves as queens and you must do this spiritually, mentally and in the physical form because in order for a real man to respect you as a woman you must respect yourself at all times make sure you examine people thoroughly before you allow someone to enter your life.

No matter what you do in life ladies never ever lose hope.

Dying In My Own Blood

I had the game locked, the world in the palm of my hand

I was the slickest roughest cat the streets ever seen

At least I thought I was until the bullet in my head told me I wasn't

It was like nothing or no one could stop me from making

My money I hustled sun up sun down until I felt the pain in my knees

I rose to the top quickly I put my work into this shit

And nobody was going to take my crown

Unaware of what was waiting for me at the end of the road

Born and raised in this same town

Trapped off by my own greed, vultures, snitches and no good niggers and bitches

This bullet hole is too deep for stitches

I look down at my family, friends and enemies

I see some crying some silently sitting full of pain I even see some happy that I am gone

Because now they can take my place get a taste of the good life

Stupid motherfucker don't even realize what he's about to do to his children and loving wife.

Yeah I grew to be the man money a house expensive trips hanging with my so called true

Homies in the club popping bottles with the finest women regulating the bars

But what did it all get me time behind bars and painful permanent scars.

In the game of crime Trust don't mean shit and you better believe your closest friend is

Really you're closest enemy

It's real in the jungle

Where no man plays fair

Shit I thought I could trust my dog but I was wrong

Shit he was the same scumbag who set me up

To catch one in the head

Same nigger knocking my girl

The last deal was supposed to go down sweet

And that's it for me I'm out

But death was my route

One shot to the head knocked off of my feet

I lay here filthy of sin, drowning like a pig in mud

Dying pitifully in my own blood.

Forgiveness, Friendships and Love:

Life is too short to let negativity come between us there are so many people praying for us to fail but you and I will never let other people control our relationship or destroy the solid bond that you and I share.

There were times we would fight fuss and cuss but through it all 2 hearts stayed united I remember how suddenly you and I went from lust to love experiencing the trials and tribulations temporary separations at times not understanding or paying attention to the important rules and regulations fighting hard not to fall victim to the evil temptations of the world.

I pray night and day to God asking him to give us the strength and patience to love one another in the proper way and when the rough storms come upon us to please shelter us from all harm and danger.

And to you my Dearest sweet heart I want you to know I love you eternally and for all the wrongs I have done the pain I have caused you I sincerely ask for your forgiveness because the friendship and love we've fought so hard to build is truly irreplaceable.

My real friends:

I appreciate my real friends forever

I can appreciate that my real friends because they just have natural love for me and they are the kind of friends who will tell you the truth rather than what you want to hear.

I love my real friends because we have grown to all be like brothers and sisters the bond we have is priceless and I would never think of hurting my true friends.

We are all different in many ways we got our issues as human beings but I believe that's what makes us so unique and allows us to be the best of friends.

There's nothing I wouldn't do for my real friends I enjoy hanging out with my friends and laughing about the old times telling the most craziest stories I even appreciate when we can all come together during the serious times and stand by one another I can't speak for others but I know God has blessed me with some real good friends.

Get Your Education:

Young Teenage boys and girls stop trying to grow up so fast enjoy being a teenager the right way take advantage of school and get an education so that you can have many opportunities think big and achieve your goals.

Those who do not go to school breaking rules at home and in school hanging out being mischievous are only headed for destruction so many of you are self-destructing by engaging in negativity you know it's wrong so why do you do it.

Listen I am not trying to preach because I know how it is to want to fit in and roll with the homies but I am here to tell you from experience when you are walking with trouble makers trouble is all you will get.

I want to see you youngsters win and what I mean is do good everyday of your life rather than to do bad there's enough of our people in jail be different rather to fill up the prisons and the cemeteries go and over flow the colleges and trade schools so many of you have enough talent to take over Hollywood and become actors and actresses bottom line is use your talents for good as you are supposed to.

It hurts to see so many teenagers losing their lives and freedom to violence mothers and fathers shedding endless tears because they lost their child to an act of violence.

Young girls feeling that it's cool to lose their virginity at the age of 15 defiling there mind and bodies thinking that it's normal to sleep with multiple guys creating a bad name for themselves before they can even graduate high school. Never sell yourself short are ladies as you should be respect yourselves and others will respect you stop trying to be grown when you don't even know how to be a child.

Last night I watched a man cry after he found out his son was wanted for a homicide and the craziest thing about it was the incident was involving two family members the son shot his cousin over a female stupid things we see and hear about everyday our young people using violence as if it is the answer when all along it's not.

Hey youngster you don't have to play the block and cut school you don't have to fight or join gang disrespect those who love you because there is nothing cool about that. I am tell your what's cool being a good person a mature young adult becoming successful the right way and another reason you don't have to go down that negative path is because I walked it already I took some punishment for you too even sat behind bars so do me a favor and do what I should of did which was be positive in make wise choices and have fun in the appropriate manner.

GOD IS ON OUR SIDE

God has joined you and I together for many reasons,

And I know that the main reason is Love,

And without you in my life,

My world does not mean anything.

Night and day,

Thoughts of you travel through my mind,

It's a blessing to be with such a woman who is understanding, caring, intelligent, and kind

And forgiving,

And whose heart is just as beautiful as her physical semblance.

This separation between you and me has opened my eyes up,

More than you could ever imagine,

The distance between us is so unfair,

I miss your smile, kiss, warm touch, and the sweet fragrance of your long jet black hair,

You are my strength and I am your strength,

I know together that you and I will make it through this storm,

This storm will soon pass,

It won't last forever,

I just want you to know,

That you will always be the one I treasure eternally.

Lock it into your mind, heart, and soul,

That I will never stop loving you no matter what problems you and I face,

We will continue to remain joined as one,

Until God says it's over,

Until then, you and I are forever.

I know at times you get angry and sad,

You probably feel like running away,

But when you get that way, do as I do,

Let God be your strength and comfort,

Because He is the only true power that can help you,

There's nothing for us to worry about,

Because I know that God is on our side,

Just know that all things take time.

Hard To Walk Away

I know at times it's hard to walk away

Especially when sin and foolish pride over power

One's mind.

But still we must not resort to violence

No man, woman or child has the right to

Take another human beings life we are all

Children of God and God does not tolerate

Or accept the fact that his children are

Destroying one another.

No one

No man, woman or child has the right to

Murder or physically harm another person.

It's time for us to stand up and be true, loyal

Loving men and follow Gods path instead of our own.

Please: If you sell drugs, make illegal money, are in a gang,

Hurt, murder, and take innocent lives

How can one say he is a man, how can a lady say

She is a woman.

He Struggles:

Born in sin to his mother he never really had his father in his life as he was supposed to.

Growing up his mother lacked morals, she was selfish and irresponsible.

At an early age he experienced a great deal of dysfunctional things that would scar him for life.

The streets in all the negative things and people in it were his role models such a shame because deep down inside he's a good guy very intelligent just does not know how to use talents in the correct way.

He learned how to hustle, scheme, manipulate and lie and so these are the tools he would use for the rest of his life God blessed him with a family but he did not appreciate nor do what a husband and father was supposed to and therefore there were more problems than good times but can he really be blamed when he did not have the proper education and tools on how to be a productive positive man how can he be a good father when he didn't have one to teach him how to be a real man, husband and a father.

Forced to carry the load often because his mother was too busy living her life he raised his siblings and made sure they had food in their bellies and clothes on their back and heat in the house by a means necessary so drugs he sold and dice he rolled.

As he got older he experienced some pain and so he medicated himself with cocaine and alcohol just to make things worse when he got mad he took it out on the ones who loved him the most only to push them away.

He has love in his heart but just does not know how to express nor give it his selfishness has caused him to lose good people, and lose good jobs somewhere along the line he stopped maturing and growing he looks at his life and begins to hate himself because he has nothing he can call his own and every man should always have his own "God bless the child who got his own" he spent his entire life trying to get over but he was only fooling himself the whole time I pray for him and ask God to keep him safe but to also help him mature and live a better life because still today he struggles.

Heaven Is My Finish Line

I am only here temporarily,

So please don't shed a tear,

When I have departed, instead be merry,

Because I have gone to a better place.

But before I go,

I must be right with the Almighty one,

This is why to some of you, I may seem different,

Well I am, because I know in order to live in God's home,

I must be right with my Father,

This is why I have not given up the fight,

To do things His way.

Trials and tribulations may cross my path,

But see, I know that God will direct my every move,

Because He controls my feet,

So I fear nothing that man or Satan the devil can do,

God is my protector.

I no longer look to man for the answers, I look to God,

I have placed myself in His care,

There's still even room for you

Because Love is something that God loves to share,

And there is room in his home for those who truly want eternal life and peace.

I'm running a race,

I am on a serious journey and there's many devils trying to stop me,

Human ones and spiritual ones but God is shining His light on me,

So nothing will stop me from going home to my Father in heaven.

I pray that my brothers and sisters will turn away from their sins,

Because the Devil only wants us to engage in his eternal suffering,

But walking the path of God will lead you to so much happiness,

A place every human being is the same.

I have learned that the land of paradise is better than any house, car, clothing, money, jewelry,

Woman or man who claims to be your friend,

But only your enemy.

So please, to all of those who are so hooked on this world,

Don't expect me to stop here,

Because this is not where it ends for me,

Heaven is my finish line.

Hey it's ok to do the right thing:

Be thankful you man for what you have God woke you up this morning your breathing so you have a second chance to get it right today you may not be a millionaire but you still must stand tall and appreciate what God has blessed you with.

Hanging out with the wrong crowd will get you nowhere them dudes are not really your friends they just around you using you but you can't see it because they making you feel like the man always riding your coattail never doing nothing for themselves come on brother open your eyes up and take a good look at what's going on the leeches rats and snakes all up under you plotting on your downfall.

I am sure you heard this all before but you will hear it until you start listening so appreciate I am willing to stay in your ear until you do what you're supposed to do and then I will back off but until then I am going to be in your ear.

How about you go back to school and get your high school diploma maybe attend college or get a good trade under your belt something you will enjoy doing and it pays good money so you never have to worry about coming to these streets.

The best thing you could ever do is stay educated it's cool to know what the streets are about but at the same time you don't have to fall victim out here put it all together school and the streets but utilize your book education to your advantage and trust me you can be the next millionaire you and your family living good with no worries at all believe in yourself even if no one else does because listen little homie you was born alone and you sure will die alone so don't be afraid to step out on faith and become a success story.

Trust me I have had my share of ups and downs but I have learned to trust in God and use my talents for what they are really worth and never let no one discourage me from achieving my goals I enjoy knowing that it is cool to do the right thing and I feel good doing the right thing it allows me to experience real happiness when I am doing the right thing in life.

And you too can have happiness you owe it to yourself so what are you waiting for get up off your butt and start claiming your good life reach for the stars and never stop you can make it brother I believe in you, you are a winner.

I Ask God

I ask God:

To please give me strength spiritually

So that my life will be more pleasant even through

The times of trouble.

To bless me with wisdom so that

I can have the knowledge to understand right

From wrong so that I don't fall into the hands of the devil.

To bless my brothers and sisters

As well with what I am praying for because

Without you in our lives God, Hell is where

We are bound to go

Please forgive not only me

But my brothers and sisters also for the sins

We have committed in the name of

Jesus I pray for your light to shine on

Us so we won't continue to walk through

This world blind.

To teach us to be patient

Loving and kind so that peace will forever

Be among us show men and women the

True way to live be joyful and learn

To always give this is what I ask God.

I Need Music

You ease my mind

And you're not hard to find

Sometime I abuse you

But I need my music…

I turn you down low and sleep

I blast you while driving my jeep

If they ever take you away I would lose it

I need music…

Everywhere I go I can hear you

You make the walls shake and glass break

I have to hear you loud you drive me wild.

I've loved you since I was a child

I like you in any form or style

I'm a junky for you

I need music…

I Pray

I pray for the people who lost their lives in the 9/11 attack

I pray for the people who were killed in Paris

I pray for any man, woman and child who was killed due to acts of violence.

I pray that God come into the minds and hearts of every human being and he removes violence from us all because this world would be much better without violence.

I pray that those who think it is okay to kill innocent people be stopped immediately I ask you now God to heal this world and make it a world of peace, unity and love.

Every human being no matter where they live deserves to feel safe no one should have to live in fear no man woman nor child should have to worry about dying why is so much war happening why can't we live in eternal peace and have nothing but good times.

I pray and I pray and I pray that we have peace all over the land because we truly need it and we need it now.

I Understand

When you need a friend, I'm here for you,

I love you more than you will ever know,

Day after day, my love for you continues to grow,

Let go of your frustration, pain, sadness, and anger,

Put those problems in God's hands,

Let him take you to a peaceful land,

I understand…

You may feel like I don't understand what you are going through,

But you're wrong,

I know what it feels like to want to give up on life and not continue on,

Don't be ashamed to cry,

Confess your sins and troubles to God,

And your days will become easy instead of hard,

I will comfort you as much as I can,

But it's a fact,

If you surrender your life to God,

You will never lose, but always win.

I used to go through frustration, pain, and sorrow,

But since I've been with the Lord,

I don't worry about yesterday or tomorrow,

I felt alone,

Trapped like I was drowning in quicksand,

And the only thing I could do was grab God's hand

He explained to me about what happens when I don't obey his commands,

So believe me,

Your problems, pain, and suffering,

I understand.

I'm Gonna Let It Shine:

I'm gonna let it shine,

I can't hold back my talent any longer,

God blessed me with this beautiful gift,

So I'm gonna let it shine;

He has chosen me to do what's right,

Get out there and fight for peace,

So the Blacks, Whites, and Hispanics

In my neighborhood can unite,

I'm gonna let it shine;

I know it's going to be hard because

So many choose the way of Satan,

Instead of God,

But I refuse to give up,

I will complete my assignment,

I'm gonna let it shine;

My gift is to talk and write positive words,

Words so strong that they will bring the world

Together,

Like love birds,

I'm gonna let it shine;

No more violence, death, and pain,

God give your children the strength to live,

As you have instructed us,

Forgive us for our sins and

Please let our talent shine…

In memory of my friend Stephen Sudden

Brother words cannot express how much I miss you man we have so many memories but still we all wish you would have never left us.

You were one of a kind brother but always a good dude who just didn't take no crap from anybody man I think about how we would turn it up in the parties some nights wilder than others always holding one another down like brothers.

I could tell so many stories but I am keep them to myself lol I am sure you are looking over us all protecting your love ones from all harm and danger just as you did when you were here on earth.

That's why it breaks my heart so much knowing you always looked out for us why did you have to be in that car why did you have to leave us but God called you home and it could not be stopped.

What I wouldn't do to talk with you and walk through the streets of Freeport with you jump in the car and ride out and find some shorty's to Mack with for the night.

To this day your respect remains you are a legend always brother and your little brother J is doing well you would be so proud of him he turned out to be a very positive productive young man.

As for me I am maintaining I have a wife and daughter and the rest of the family is alright you wouldn't believe I am a counselor working with the kids in our neighborhood I finally published a few books and I am currently in school to enhance my skills and work ethic that's the best way to do things now a days bro well I could go on and on but I will end with these words Stephen Sudden better known as Poppa you are truly missed until we meet again my friend please continue to watch over us all you will always be loved and missed Rest In Heaven My Friend.

In memory of our brother Ray Shawn:

Brother you are truly missed but trust and believe we have not forgotten you we laugh much about you and some of the things you used to do wow so many memories you left us with but still and all your Harris Ave crew still wishes you were here.

You had the heart of a lion, never back done from anybody and for sure dudes knew to respect it I guess that's why they would always try to get slick and not want to fight you fair but it's all good because we always was there to hold you down.

I wonder what life would be like for you if you were still here I think about how you used to climb the trees to the highest branch and how we would ride bikes to the recreation center and sometime sneak in lol the good times.

I reminisce on how we would drink our 40 ounces of beer or slide off to the bootlegger for some mad dog 20/20 yeah we was some wild boys but it's all love bro I want you to know we are all doing good some ups and downs here and there but we are good living life working hard and taking care of our families.

You are forever in our hearts bro for sure gangster we know you are in heaven watching over us and for that we are thankful, we miss you Ray Shawn Rest in Heaven brother.

Life or death which do you chooses? You wonder why I am asking this question well simply because it seems that my black brothers don't care about dying and going to prison,

Brothers have children out here in the world but will put hustling and females before their child or children and then get mad when your child's mother hit you with child support or deny you the right to be with your child/children,

Change is good so don't be afraid to change for the better too many of us are losing we are killing one another and being killed by others it's time we

Wake up and make a difference so that our children will have a better chance at life break the cycle stop passing down the same misery that has destroyed you if you really see yourself as a man,

Than do what a real man would do and step up to the plate get a job be responsible and if you have a child or more than one child learn to be a great father I wouldn't care if you needed parenting classes it's alright at least you have the courage to learn the skills to be the best parent you can be,

I know it's hard out here but it's even more harder when you have to do a bid and come home and start from the bottom again and some of my brothers repeat this cycle over and over until they end up rotting away it does not have to be like this brothers there is always a better way.

Its ok to get up and go to work for what you want the same way you put that energy into making it to the top in the streets you can do that by starting your own business or becoming the head man in charge at a big time incorporation you will never know unless you try so what you waiting for get out there and start to achieve your goals and become a success story.

So again I ask you which do you choose life or death I hope by the time you finish reading this your answer will be to choose life stay involved in positive things and build your foundation to be solid as a mountain you can do it brothers I am praying for you all to overcome the madness that has been holding you back break the chains and don't look back at what you used to be because God is working on you renewing you forget those who refuse to change you have to make it to your blessing because you deserve it.

From the writer: Donald D Robinson/ A-K-A Pop

Pease and blessings my brothers

Lights Flashing

Lights flashing

Eyes blinking

People thinking different about you.

You shouting against the pain.

Again people like to think you're insane.

The main reason is

You can't get your head straight.

It's really spinning around.

It hurt real badly.

You aren't mad, you're just a

Bit sad with your life.

You just might keep your eyes

Closed let the light flash.

Mother's Love:

Whenever it seemed like the world was against me, no matter what the circumstances seemed to be you always stood strong by my side.

For the times I acted out of character and ignored the good things about life you taught me I apologize and I know I may not have always shown it but you mean the world to me.

If it were up to me I would give you the universe I owe you my life, especially for all the times I made you want pull out your hair scream and curse, I just want you to know that you are my best friend and I love you.

Without a second thought you are the true meaning of love and respect, you gave me life which is the greatest gift I could ever have so there's no need for me to judge or wonder to myself do you love me because you have sacrificed and bent your back for me in more ways than one.

I really can't explain how it feels to have such a beautiful mother whose heart is more valuable than diamonds, silver and gold you are god's blessing. From the heavens up above sweet and gentle as a dove there's nothing greater on this earth to me than my mother's love…

My Beautiful Black Brothers and Sisters

Let us learn to love and respect each other again;

Why can't that sister stop selling her body for money?

How come that brother is going back to prison for selling drugs;

Why is grandma always getting stuck with her daughter and son's children?

In some cases why are the children taking care of the parents;

What's going on in the schools… why are our children not taking advantage of school like they should;

Why my neighborhood got be labeled the hood;

Little Pee Wee is not crazy, he's growing up without a father, he's just misunderstood but can you really blame him for being angry? He wants his dad.

God I cry out to you on my knees begging you please open up the black man and black woman's eyes to your word. Let our hearts desire you, God. Please save my beautiful black brothers and sisters.

My thoughts of the world today:

It seems as if the world is at its worst could this finally be the end?

Everywhere I turn there is war, war in our communities war in other countries hell even war amongst family members.

Going to war what does it accomplish the only thing that I have learned and seen that war only causes more pain, sadness and anger nothing good comes from war.

I pray for the world because we need your help God too many innocent lives have been taken for foolishness so much negativity has invaded our land God was all this madness supposed to be part of the plan.

Young boys walking around with guns selling drugs and banging losing their lives to the penitentiary or an early grave neglecting education refusing discipline dancing with sin until it permanently destroys them.

Father God please forgive us and I ask that you help us let us stop the war instill in us to show love and not hate I just don't understand why you allow so much violence to go on church folk say you have a plan but I am tired of all of the senseless killings so I vow to take a stand and encourage people all over the world to stop being violent learn to be peaceful at all times.

On a negative path:

Young boy standing on the block

Selling what the feigns call B-Rock,

Stunting with a chrome 9 knowing he

Wont shoot nobody because he not really

Trying to go to jail no knowledge of the meaning

Keep it real.

He doesn't even realize he is his own worst enemy

Choosing to dwell in the streets with the beasts

Teaching him to fail, thinking going to jail will

Strengthen his level of street cred and respect
how foolish he really is.

A word from the wise young player I am one who has been through all that you're doing young boy use your mind for you not against you go to school get an education and make yourself become a positive success story it's enough black men sitting in prison or laying in the cemetery why don't you be different and do things the right way.

You can have all the money in the world but without education you will end up broke faster than you can believe you probably don't have no money stashed away for an attorney in case you get locked up you too busy being flashy spending all your cash only to come right back to the same stinking street corner that will only be the death of you or cause you to spend years up north somewhere.

That street mentality won't get you far the streets will slowly break you down and leave you for dead there's some real lions in the jungle that will rip you apart just on GP, don't be afraid to ask for help I rather see you working a 9-5 than to be serving 25 to life for some foolishness.

If you think them clowns you rolling really got your best interest trust in believe as soon as you get arrested they will turn on you as if there were no tomorrow and your right hand man will be sleeping with your girl think it's a game if you want to young blood its cold, dark and lonely when you sitting in that cell.

Be inspired to learn and grow stay educated and keep your mind on positive things knowledge is power as they say but the longer you stay out here playing in the streets living negative your pushing yourself closer to your last day stand strong and fight through the storm ask to protect you trust in him and he will take care of you.

Please listen to my words I speak what I speak because I know from experience what fake people and these mean streets can do to a man's life young brother you can be anything you want to be if you allow yourself to be patient and humble I hope you get it together and go back to school and really do good with your life you deserve to live a beautiful life.

Peace:

I would like to ask my brothers and sisters in my community to please stop the violence the senseless killings the unnecessary fighting and ignorance let us put it to rest.

Little boys are watching us men and what are we showing them be sure to show them positivity at all times we must not portray negative behavior disrespect our women and commit crimes because they are only going to follow our wicked ways if we are not carful to build the young ones up in the appropriate manner.

The children our children your children all children deserve a greater environment then we had let's give them the serenity that they need in order for them to live healthy lives because the children surely are our future.

We need to hear peace in our music promote peace on T.V. and educate our schools on how to promote peace on a daily basis our children need to feel safe in school at home and in the community.

We need God in our hearts and minds every day every night 24/7 we must pray for peace so I ask God to take away the hate and the violence the drugs and all that is bad for us and replace it with goodness so that we can once again have true happiness here on earth as we should.

Yes let us have everlasting Peace within ourselves
and have respect and peace for others.

Secrets are hidden within his hart,

Angry and confused trying to wash away the pain,

With drugs, alcohol, and sex;

But, the nightmare still remains constantly,

Blaming himself for what happened to his best friend,

He feels it should be him locked behind bars;

See, his friend should not have got caught with that gun,

It should have never been in the house at all;

Looking forward to better days to spend with you, my friend,

Waiting for you to be free,

Free from the belly of the beast,

Because a man like you should be home with your family;

I wish you would have never taken the gun with you that night,

I understand how you felt but,

We could have handled things a better way,

I'm glad no one got hurt,

But sad you are back in the Devil's hole,

I pray for you, my friend,

I miss you and I love you.

So you want to be tough:

I have seen this picture a million times and more young boy like you disrespecting your mother angry because daddy is not around so you start rolling with the thugs in the hood carrying around hurt and displaced anger quicker to love a stranger because you can careless about your family trying to figure it all out on your own but many miles from being grown.

Don't get offended youngster just listen up and listen good see your anger is understandable but if you do not challenge it in a positive direction you are going to end up in a lot of trouble so do yourself a favor and smarten up and be easy back away from them streets before you end up locked up or dead or permanently in a wheel chair unable to move trust me little homie eventually you gonna keep playing with fire until you lose.

The other day you felt it would be cool to jump that kid from your school he was minding his business not causing you any harm but you wanted to show others around you that you were tough fronting just to make a name for yourself but look at you now charged with a gang assault serving a dime for nearly killing that kid the time slowly tearing your part as your cell mate takes advantage of you in every way possible now you want to go home the gates close lights out and your pants cum down while his penis is in your mouth as the other dude greases you up and begins to please himself by pushing in and out of you never once did you think this would happen to you but it is and there's nothing you can do about it I think it's best for you to request for protective custody because the rate you're going your either going to hang up or be forced to take your abusers life damn how would your homies feel knowing that you are the prison whore just because you wanted to be tough look where it got you.

I know my words are harsh and some may get mad but this is reality and it can happen to anybody because it has now I don't wish bad things on anyone but sometimes people put themselves in bad situations never thinking about what can happen these streets and the prisons are filled with ruthless animals that will devour you if you play in these streets you have to be more an animal you can never hesitate to take your enemy out on site the consequence are serious and many are not built for it so the best thing you youngsters could do is be smart get an education and stay out of trouble the time the state and feds are handing out is not a game its real so why don't you keep it real and not end up another statistic as many of us have and you may not get your manhood taken but just being locked up for a long period of time unable to grow mentally and achieve your goals is bad enough you want to be tough become the next Barack Obama or the next high profile doctor, lawyer or architect maybe the next incredible famous athlete anything but wanting to be the next gangster because all the gangsters end up dead or behind bars but the choice is yours which one will you choose.

Just some words from the messenger.

Stop being a Thot:

So you got some people fooled portraying to be a hard working loving caring mother when really deep down inside you have no self-control at all.

As soon as pay day come you club hopping getting drunk twirking that ass for drinks in the bar screwing different men every chance you get but you want to be respected who is going to respect you if you don't respect yourself.

A beautiful woman you are but ratchet to the core bad mouthing your baby daddy spreading lies never once taking a look at yourself 3 different baby fathers but you don't have no issues your life style is disgusting but you can't see with your eyes closed head in the fog for once in your life wake up and change your ways so that you can have better days.

You want a man to love you but you don't love yourself because if you did you wouldn't be opening your legs up to every man who runs game on you if you had a strong mind and knew how to carry yourself as a mature classy woman you would never have a nasty label on you but class and maturity is what you lack.

I pray for you sister I pray that you change because if you don't you're going to lose a lot more than yourself respect sooner or later your family and friends will see who you really are and what's really bad is when your children begin to witness how trashy you are how are you going to explain your behavior to them oh I know your one of those mothers to say it's none of your business I am grown that's just your poor excuse of a woman defense mechanism wow so many of you have this mentality.

Woman like you make all the good women look bad but I salute the Good woman who carry themselves as ladies maintaining respect and class for themselves keep doing your thing because you deserve it. Real women don't bring shame upon themselves or their children but you got a lot to learn shorty so many of you woman have a lot to learn.

But I can't blame you because men are responsible for this problem we have because so many men disrespect women so much today some women feel it is ok like its normal well it's never normal for a man to disrespect a woman in any way what so ever.

To the men out there who have little girls remember we must lead by an example because we know damn well we are not going to tolerate some clown disrespecting our daughters so straighten up and stop disrespecting our women out here even if a woman has no respect encourage her to be respectful you never know how that may help her clean up her act and stop being a THOT……

STOP THE GANG WAR:

I remember when the two of you used to be friends how you'll use to play together, go to the same baby sitter, sleep at each other's house went to junior high school together shared clothes so how could you let a color and negativity of money, guns, and the streets take away your beautiful friendship.

Hate and death is what you now share because he represents red and you rock blue. Was it ever really supposed to get this crazy? Look how our communities have changed.

Innocent children are being killed getting caught in the cross fire, who are you to determine who lives and dies, you are trapped in a world of evilness, and ignorance it's sad that you can't open your eyes and realize the damage you're doing to yourselves and others.

What's it going to take for you to stop a sharp bullet or knife? Do you truly know what a gangster is? My definition of a Gangster is a man who does not kill a man for colors, money, drugs or anything at all. A real Gangster will learn to reason… Now I know sometimes you can't always reason and things happen, but what we are doing today is uncalled for.

Furthermore I feel that if you're so Gangster you should be providing a roof over your families head educating your sons and daughters about the dangers of the street treating that lady of your life like the queen she is.

Don't look for excuses to kill a person or to say this is why I gang bang because there are many people who had it rough who found a safe way out of the life of crime who was able to go a positive route.

You young boys out there on the block call yourselves holding it down being thugged out for your man but when shit hits the fan I don't see your home busting his gun or coming to bail you out of jail.

Now look who is doing the time crying like a bitch because you know you played yourself about to do 33-life for shooting a cat from the other side. Ask yourself is losing your life to the system really worth it?

Brothers and sisters too because you'll down just as well don't justify the systems plan and trap yourself off only for them to make money off of you for the rest of your life because they love it when you catch a case they look for those of you who sell drugs, carry guns, and murder people... violence, to some in the government is their bread and butter, a real pay day.

I think about how my man shot who he thought was in a gang just turned out that the kid was not a gang member at all. He was neural now my dog is going to prison for the next 20 years and that innocent kids family still wants him to do more time they feel 20 years is not enough look at what's going on.

It's never too late to turn away from this negative life of gang violence and horrible crime. Why keep playing Satan's game he will only lead you to misery and death tell me how would you feel if someone took your sister or brother's life and they had plans to go to college or get married but it could never happen because your gang banging is why they lost their life. I bet you don't think about your loved ones do you?

This morning I prepare myself for one more funeral this is the 8th one this month and I am only in the middle of October. My friend was shot in the head 3 times because he chose to be a gangster and disrespect people. But the question I ask is that how many more of my people have to die? FATHER I pray to you and ask please stop the GANG WAR...

The Realest Words I Ever Wrote:

Many people have a problem with a Gay or Lesbian individual and it is actually understandable, just as some people have issues with drug addicts or convicts and prostitutes and a racist organization and so on.

My view of a Gay man or a Lesbian woman is this you are still a human being therefore conduct yourself as an appropriate person, who am I to judge anyone when I am not a perfect man.

Do I feel at times the media and T.V. shows go overboard with promoting Gay and lesbian relationships and sex yes I do but as I said that's my own personal opinion.

Do I have Gay and Lesbian friends or family members yes I do and I have much respect for them. There sexual preference does not make them who they are there character as a human being is what defines them.

There is much that we say is wrong and what is right I say all that we feel is wrong put it and Gods hands because even in the bible the word tells us to show love and kindness and not take matters into our own hands.

There's enough hate in the world for many different things and that's the problem hate hating a person because they are Gay, Lesbian, black, white Hispanic or because they are poor or too rich or because of their religion I wonder if people see how ridiculous this is.

I don't like a lot of things that people in the world do or that the government does but face it we cannot stop it, many people have Gay and lesbian people in their families. Just as we have a drunk a drug addict a thief a liar and so on and so on, let's just be thankful that we are still breathing and therefore we must focus on ourselves and worry about making ourselves better. I pose a question if your child or best friend was Gay or Lesbian would you disown him or her I know many people would let me also ask what if you had a terminal sickness how would you feel if people turned them back on you.

I am just asking a realistic question and touching on a topic that most would not a person should never be judged because of their past, nor their religion, sex or criminal history or what their nationality is I judge people based on their manners and there heart it will define if a person is good or bad.

To My Brothers:

I remember how I was standing on the block pumping crack and cocaine 100 miles an hour destroying my people and quick to start some drama just because I felt I could but deep down inside I was miserable and troubled.

Picking up bad habits such as being violent to people even the women that I was deeply involved with disrespecting them verbally and physically thinking I was being a man and in control and in reality had control of nothing not even myself.

Yeah I learned a lot out of living an unhealthy lifestyle how can I ever forget being stabbed and getting jumped and having people wanting to set me up and send me to jail or the time I heard so and so wanted to kill me or how can I forget being arrested and having to do that county bullet I will never forget the pain I went through because I was trying to be the man on the streets.

Today I enjoy being the man for my family working hard to give my wife and daughter a better life and to be there for my mother and brother in the right manner.

Little hustlers out there on them corners today do you really think you coming up off them grams man that game is played out you weak home boy try working and getting yours the right way but I can dig it I really can't judge you for doing you I just know from experience where your headed and your path is very dangerous full of life threatening consequences.

Wasting time smoking weed and popping bottles selling drugs while time passes you by still with no to show for it living fairy tales you a nickel and dime hustler broke ass buster what's really good with you my boy you slipping faster and faster as the days go by.

Are you selling the drugs because it looks to me like the drugs are selling you I'm not trying to preach to you my man I am just dropping a jewel on you because as I said I know from experience what lies ahead for you and it is nothing nice my friend so wise up and get on the right path because the journey your walking never leads happy ending so I say to my brothers please wake up and begin to change your ways life is full of struggles, trials and tribulations but as long as you pray and believe in God he will always make a way for you just have faith and do the right thing.

To My Father:

If we never speak again in life I want you to know I apologize for what occurred between you and I there is so much I want to say and I may not get to say it all but my there is a big part of my heart that hurts.

Family I ask what does it mean to you because you instilled in me to look out for family and a be family orientated but it seems as if you yourself do not know what family is all about and how a man is supposed to value and protect his family.

As I provide and set the foundation for my own family what I realize on a daily basis is that as a husband and father it's not about what my family can do for me it's about what I must do for my family in order to ensure they have a happy life.

I learn that I cannot call myself a man let alone a husband and father if I am causing more bad than good for my family and playing the game of lying and cheating being selfish always wanting to please my flesh.

If you ever read this you might not like the words I speak but I speaking from my heart because this is how I feel, my father you will always be and your son I will always be that's never going to change I just wish you would have never took me or your family for granted the blain ten disrespect was just going on far too long how did you let yourself go and fall into another trap trying to play the game only to lose you should of known better because you been there more times than one but who am I to judge to each his own I just know the way you live and the way you are I will be different and for the bad ways I have like you I just pray daily for God to remove them so I can be a better man and not a better man than you just a better man in general.

Part of me despises you but there is a part of me that loves you and I want to say I love you more than I despise you I really wish it could be different even wish you was still here but you're not so I have to move forward with my life what's done is done.

What I would like to ask you is a few questions

Do you know God blessed you with a beautiful wife and two great sons?

Why would you base your family and relationship with your wife what you thought it should be

How could you turn your back on your family and always choose trash over your family did we ever come first in your life

Do you even appreciate the things we have all done for you especially your son are going down a negative path to help you?

Are you really an ungrateful selfish man these are just questions I would ask you if you were standing in front of me and are you really happy where you are and are you happy with the things you have done.

I go hard in life because I don't want mines to be like yours and you or anyone can take this personal I am my own man stating how I feel you may view things different but I know the truth and as I said it is what it is because I am always going to make sure your wife my mother is good whether you're here or not because that's the man I am it's the man you raised me to be.

I hope you are doing well and that your health is good and for what it's worth I never meant to wish any bad on you or say I wished you were dead my anger got the best of me and I erupted like a volcano the anger was burning inside of me for much too long but at the end of the day 2 wrongs don't make a right.

I would have never took you for granted or took advantage of you the way you did us I understand you were raised in a bad way I understand you had it hard but the day God blessed you with my mother and you had me and my brother you should have realized right then and there that God was on your side and all you had to do was be a man but how could you be that man we wanted you to be when you never really knew how because you didn't have a man to teach you or give you the proper tools to do exactly what a man should do.

I guess taking the coward way out was easy for you to do that won't be me and I will help my brothers not to be cowards as well life gets hard throws some blows but real man stands in fight they never run. I am at a point where I am educating myself on something's.

Such as if I have a problem with my wife I won't run to another female if I am having any kind of issue financially with family or anything I am going to deal with it appropriately.

You have done a lot of harm to your family you have caused a lot of pain on people due to your own selfishness, anger and hurt I hope one day you will see that and really be a man and give effort to correct things before it is too late and again you may not like what I am saying if you read this but you need to hear it I will never stop loving you no matter if the communication never exist again but I will always love you and from my heart to yours I hurt inside I pray for you daily and I am sorry for my anger, hurt and violent outburst.

Maybe one day you and I will make a mends and strengthen our bond that once was beautiful I wish you no harm just the peace and happiness you deserve.

My Siblings:

I want you all to know I love you with all my heart through the years circumstances have put a gap in our relationship we are similar in many ways but also different it doesn't matter though because I love you all the same.

We are at a point in our lives where we must really stay connected; life is too short as we see we are in the grown up stage of life we have children and other responsibilities so it's important that we do the right thing at all times.

There have been times I may not have displayed the proper behavior and although I am the oldest I am capable of making poor choices and mistakes but it does not change the fact that I would go to the bitter end for you we are family forever.

Sometimes I ask myself why did our lives have to be so twisted and complicated but that's not our fault but I won't touch on that doesn't make sense to point the finger and throw blame what we must do is move forward and make the best out of our lives because the most beautiful thing has happened it that is we are brothers and sisters and no one can take that away from us not ever.

To my younger brothers I want us all to be out here enjoying life going on trips and having fun building a life time of memories relaxing at the backyard cook outs and spending time with one another as much as we can.

I pray for my family on a daily basis because I want you all to have a great life filled with happiness and peace at times I feel alone because I miss my brothers I just want to go ride and kick it with you'll and talk about all that's been going on I just need my brothers and sisters to know we are one and I truly, truly love you all.

To Whom It May Concern

Born into a world of sin do I want out or will I stay in, my first Love was a 38 Revolver and an Ounce of Crack so deep into this game for me there is no turning back.

Living on anger hurt and pain my life feels like an Eternal nightmare, heart scarred since birth hell on earth sometimes I wonder what life is really worth. Pimps, pushers, prostitutes crooked men dressed in expensive suits; gangster's rocking all black with timberland boots.

I'm just a nigger from the hood misunderstood up to know good looking for a way out but everywhere I turn all doors are locked frustration Increases causing my mind to stay blocked how long will you keep me in these chains should I let this bullet splatter my brains?

Together you and I are Stronger:

I know that this is hard on you and you are doing the best you can to stand your ground, raising our children, working and maintaining the bills.

I want to say truly from my heart I apologize for my negative ways and actions for all the hurt I've caused you and our children.

Not being able to talk to you hold you in my arms and spend quality time with you and our beautiful children hurts me more than you could ever imagine, night and day. I beat myself down for my foolish acts how could I put a negative life style of misery and pain before my wife and children.

I'm reaching out to you because I'm hurting and I am tired of causing havoc on my loved ones and myself you are the only I truly have in my corner the only one who understand me.

I'm fighting hard day after day to get my life in order so I can truly be the man I am the man you and our children need, right now I feel so far away from you not only physically but mentally and I know honestly it should not be this way.

I know you're angry and you have every right but please don't let your anger over power your love. You are a beautiful, intelligent, warm hearted woman with style and I love you and we should never stop or lack communicating, encouraging and most of all turn our backs on one another as I said you're all I got.

I know I haven't been the best husband lover or friend but that old me is dead because I can't let the old me continue to destroy my life and the people around me who I love the most.

No one is perfect, I wish I was tough at times because the problems I'm dealing with would not exist, but I'm g0ing to keep pressing on and put my faith in God because he will truly help me to become the man I need to be for you and the children and help me to turn away from the negative things that are holding me down.

I pray that you and I still have a band that's unbreakable you know really inseparable because no matter what I will never stop loving you, I need you in more ways than one I can't live life like this any longer, I want to make our love last I really miss your friendship, encouragement and gorgeous smile, we can work through this by standing by one another because together you and I are stronger…

Truly My Lady:

It took some time for me to realize that you are the only woman in this world for e. I was strong enough to fight through all the distractions, rumors and wicked lies. What people don't understand is that I am one hundred percent a man and I know my woman and I guess they're jealous of the love you and I share.

When I look at you I see heaven in your eyes. You're the woman every man dreams of and I'm blessed to call you my wife to be with… Someone who knows me inside and out your friendship and love is my food and I can never get enough I'm honored to have to have you in my life.

I give you my tears, heart, joy and even my last breath you are that special person I've been waiting to love, hold, and touch. To create a family with and through all the difficult times I promise that my love will remain strong no matter how rough the winds, thunder storms and rain may get I will always love you unconditionally and do whatever I have to do to take away your pain.

I look forward to our afternoon walks through the park our late night romantic talks and especially when we turn out the lights put on some Marvin Gaye light a candle and make love I cherish those moments just I cherish you for being the beautiful woman that you are. You wonder why I constantly wear a smile on my face well it's because I can tell by the way you love me that you are truly my lady.

Untitled

Times are getting so hard, my people

Have been hit with emotional pain

Left mentally scarred;

My mind is flooded with so many

Get rich schemes, but I fall back

And catch myself because I realize

I'm chasing dreams;

Regretting getting these felonies

Feeling foolish, no one understands I

Made a bad choice, I just need a second

Chance to make my life right;

I guarantee I won't fail, no more

Baggies, no more digital scales, I'm stepping

Up to the plate like a true man and for

The first time in my life I'm going to keep

It real;

My plan is to work hard, live honest, and

Achieve my goals. I know I'll have some highs

And lows may even have to eat a few painful

Blows but I will rise to the top and when

I get there; God is who will get all the glory

Because it is he who saved me.

Violence, is it worth it?

Violence- what is its purpose and what point does it prove? To take another human beings life is truly a sin. So many of my brothers and sisters young and old are either killing or being killed because of pure foolishness.

The man who took another man's life because of money and drugs has also lost his life hit with seventy five years of prison time and day after day his guilt is severely destroying him, now ask yourself was it worth it, Is it ever worth it brother and sisters pay attention to what I am saying because madness like this happens every day. I mean Damn just think about what you have and who loves you think about the consequences before you make that bad choice to end up standing in front of the judge who is not going to care about you at all never wanting to give you a drop of mercy because you had none for others. Don't be like the one who gave up his family for negativity be smart trust me it is ok to do the right thing so that you can live a peaceful life.

A woman lost her life today as she stood waiting for the bus, the gang wearing blue attempted to shoot the man who represents red, but instead they shot an innocent woman leaving her dead. Now what is going to happen to her children and her devoted husband, I'm sure her killers never thought about that. Open your eyes and realize truly what is right and what is wrong and ask yourself is it really worth it?

We live in insane times, our children addicted to gangs, drugs, and committing crimes. George Bush, the Devil, got us twisted losing our minds.

What NOT are you doing, is the question I ask. Oh you don't understand? Let me explain. Why won't you let me explain and take care of our family? Why when you get knocked and go to jail you don't have a positive Plan B?

Why don't you respect yourself or your lady? What's really good with you? A million excuses to be the government's mule. That shit isn't gangster. In, out of jail, thinking you're hardcore, don't even know the difference between a real woman and a whore. Nah, son, you the fool.

I look at you, homie, and say, "not me my mind is too strong!" For the devil's trap, the only hole I want to be stuck in is some beautiful queen's gap.

Sounds crazy but I'm just keeping it real because I know from experience when you locked in that cage it paralyzes your soul, leaving you unable to breath, loneliness is all a man will feel.

Listen to my words; I know they may be sharp, ripping through your skin. I'm just being honest, like a true friend should and I hope what I am saying to you sinks deep into your mind, trust me nowadays people that speak the truth are hard to find.

WE NEED TO COMMUNICATE

Our lack of communication is truly disturbing,

I'm stuck with worries, I wonder if you are safe,

I wonder whether or not if you're mentally and physically healthy,

I wonder if you are thinking about me as much as I think of you.

I don't matter if we write or talk over the phone,

I need to know that you are OK,

And also know how your days are going,

I'm reaching out to you because you're special to me,

And the love in my heart that I have for you is deeper than you would ever know.

Communication is what will help us grow as friends and lovers,

Communication will also bring understanding to our relationship,

I would do anything for you,

These days, weeks and months are lonely without you,

We need to communicate.

I just want you to know, I love you,

Thoughts of you are in my mind,

My spirit feels you and I need your love and friendship,

I say these words to you with all honesty,

We need to communicate.

Welcome To Harris Ave also known as H- Block

On this block you will see and find that we are one unit and if we have anyone to try to disrespect that posing as an imposter he or she will be removed.

Let me explain a bit deeper about what I mean see we show love over here but we get in over here as well so don't think you can come on our block and front because you can get the business it trust me it will not be nice so let's keep it all love.

It's only right for me to represent my block you can catch me over here any time chilling and vibing with my brother Drizzy or the Nation Friday nights you might catch me with my man Moto or my man Frankie Aka Big Just and that's just a few of my brothers because our squad is deep although we all are older now we still hold it down around here trust in believe the last chump that came through fronting the nation had to put him on his face it's not a game if you come looking for a fight because somebody from around here going to give you what you asking for and that ass whipping will not be nice so again I warn you walk through this block in peace.

I love my block nearly 30 years strong we keep it tight on all corners we seen a lot go down around here from state cases to fed cases shoot outs and police chases and crazy fights but at the end of the day me and my Harris Ave crew we stay united because all we got is us and I can't forget about the older brothers who were out here before us holding the block down such as Big Tamel may the God rest in peace and I can't forget about Starmel, Justice, Everlasting, Elevation, Marco and Lance and many more who are a part of this block always holding it down.

And don't let me forget my man Freaky he out here with us for real and he will definitely hold it down because that what's it about H-block strong for life you won't find no niggers over here just real men who look out for each other over on this side.

The ladies no what time it is with us Harris ave boys many have fell victim but it's all love we know we a different breed around here ladies we will romance you in all kind of ways and then go our separate ways lol it's all fun and love though on the real we just them H- block boys.

What Ever It Takes:

I am not a man with super powers and I never present myself as superman but I will do whatever it takes to encourager and up lift my brothers and sisters to live a healthy life.

I may not always say the right words or do the right thing but I never give up on myself nor others I will always encourage men women and children to be peaceful and love themselves I will encourage education and unity as well as love.

Today I choose to be peaceful and forgive because God has forgiven me and spared me many times and I know that God wants me to do the right thing at all times so I give the effort to do so I trust in God at all times.

Life may attempt to beat me down and my family and friends may even turn against me but through it all I have God he is all I need I get my strength from God because at the end of the day my peace of mind and happiness is a blessing to have therefore it is only right that I share God's word with others and while I am living here on earth do my best to assist with healing all of my brothers and sister s who are hurting spiritually, mentally and physically.

The world we live in could really be better if we get rid of the hatred and the unnecessary violence our children deserve to have a future that exist of peace, respect, love and unity I ask God every day to make the world a better place for every man, woman and child I hope that he answers my prayer.

What help do we get in here:

They say they have assistance for us to not repeat the cruel cycle of coming back and forth to prison but where's the help at counselors in here don't help us the guards in some cases are worse than the prisoners.

I don't understand with all the money these facilities make why we don't get the proper help we need but they allow negative things to go on or turn a blind eye to it all we are is livestock to them working for pennies but I can't blame them but so much because we do it to ourselves when we go out and commit crimes.

Foolish people glorify prison as if it was something cool I never have been proud of wearing handcuffs and doing time in jail a real man would never even allow himself to think that being incarcerated is something to brag about because the truth is when a man or woman is sitting locked behind bars we are not feeling as we are in control or we are winning hell no we are feeling ashamed and want to be free out in the world with our family and friends.

I remember when I had to patiently wait for my release date the things that I witnessed which I won't mentioned was truly disturbing I thank God for keeping me mentally strong as well as physically strong and I did not succumb to any negativity while I was behind the wall.

Seeing men come back from court with eyes full of tears because they blew trial and got hit with life or they were in on a minor case but then got into a situation that cost them to get more time than they originally had the pain that prison dishes out is not cool.

My negative choices have led me here I admit but now it's up to me to make the changes that need to be made so that I don't ever come back here again this is just one place I am not feeling hell no not at all.

Just the other day an inmate attempted to kill himself with only 3 days left of his bid he found out his wife cheated on him with his best friend the madness that goes through one's mind but maybe it had to be this way because this man probably would have killed both of them including himself thankfully he is going to be alright and I see he has family to support him but there are times where some are not that fortunate many men and women have killed themselves in here for all kind of horrific reasons.

There is no help in here there is no love no one to trust everyday spent in here you have to be on point so you don't get violated in anyway if there is anything I can say to my brothers out there who have never been to jail or prison don't start now if you're on a negative path get off it before it takes your freedom away find something better to do with your time my brothers if no one told you are to beautiful and strong minded of a man to be wasting years behind bars so please make a difference and stop making that place a revolving door the state has made enough money off of us.

Thankful to be free I am staying strong so that I never go back to that terrible place I want to be successful raise my daughter and spend time with my wife in the right way I never want to put them through a life like that no not at all so I pray for the strength to stay straight and work hard and put my faith in God because I know he will take care of my every need and make sure my wife and daughter will be alright.

When I look into her eyes...

I can see that love is truly in her heart; her tender touch is strong enough to move mountains her beautiful smile has enough power to light up the world. Could it be that I have found that special one?

Sitting under the moon lite holding her in my arms assuring her that she's safe from all harm and danger. To never stop loving her constantly flows through my head. I just want to give her everlasting affection and a friendship that could never be replaced, caress her mind, body and soul until the day I die. She's the woman who deserves to be treated like a queen continuously, keeping our love brand new every day for the rest of our lives. Dedicating myself to you 100% no half stepping nothing in between.

WHO AM I?

I hate peace I hate higher power I hate anyone who
Loves his fellow brother or sister to all who come in
Contact with me I wish you death and suffering.

I enjoy seeing Fathers and mothers crying filled with
Anger it thrills me to see your sweet children being
Carried away in a hearse and families torn apart.

I come into the minds of many but I am quicker to
Manipulate teenagers or those who are sincerely weak
I have killed millions and am very pleased I'll sneak
Up on you when you least expect it I am in the blood
Of every race I have no love for Gods children I
Destroy communities, countries and households I am
Evil.

I love it when the bloods and Crips kill one another
And the Latin kings destroy the MS 13 I don't care if
Innocent children lose their lives they should not have
Been in my way I destroy all that is good even as I
Speak to you right now I am planning a thousand more
Funerals.

I need more guns and knives in your children's hands
I get a kick out of seeing your sons and daughters go
To jail for the rest of their lives it's my duty to make
Sure they rot in hell.

It's true I am very well hated and I always show up
Unexpectedly but you choose to have me so many
Have chosen me over reality and peace.

I thank the parents who are too busy getting high, out
Partying or just don't care at all to educate their
Children about me, you know those of you who let
Your children roam the streets at all hours of the night
Leaving them to fin for themselves feeling unloved.

Pushing them into gangs, drugs, committing horrific crimes
That only causes them to lose their freedom it just makes me
Happy to see people hurt and I will stop at nothing to harm the
Entire world if you don't want me in your life or in your mind stop
Using me when you get angry I bet your trying to figure out just who
I am.

I am just out right evil and I do not care because of you wicked foolish people in the world
I am growing bigger than ever because so many of you constantly use me to
Deal with your issues but your so damn foolish because I only make your troubles
worse oh you still want to know who I am allow me to introduce myself my name
Is Violence you know me I am the one who gets into the minds of the week and cause?
People to hurt and kill one another such as right now I am in this man's head causing
him to beat his wife even better I have a teenager about to shoot another teenager over
a girl yup I am good old violence.

Oh and don't think I only target men didn't I mention before I destroy women as well
I have made females kill and hurt each other many times bottom line is I am the worlds
Worse night mare and I do not plan on leaving until all of you are dead and permanently
Suffering. It's like they say on your wedding day until death do us part that's the only
way you will ever get rid of me unless of course you are strong enough to control your
temper when you get angry.

So until we meet again and believe me many of you I will meet again I wish you all
eternal pain and suffering I am Violence.

Willing to Learn

Unable to read or write

Disconnected from education;

Struggling just to count to 50

The alphabet, he can only sing them A to P;

Tired of the other kids teasing him

An educated man is what he desires to be;

Was it his fault mama never let him

Sound out the words during a bed time story;

Truth is she never had time for a child like him

Did he do something wrong;

Does she neglect him because his father doesn't?

Want her anymore, I wonder if she realizes he

Left him as well;

All he ever wanted was an education, a high

School diploma possibly a college degree,

Be all he can be like the men in the army;

He prays for knowledge because he is willing to learn.

You are My Everything:

For you and I this has been a very rough year but together we made it through, because our love never stopped;

It didn't get weaker but only stronger when others turned their back on me and life treated me unfair I can honestly say that you were the only one who stayed by my side and told me not to worry, because mother will always be here and mother will always care.

When I was afraid and got weak your love encouraged me to do better you said son keep your head up.

You taught me how to truly be a man and today I owe it to you because today strong is how I stand.

I will always love you whether I'm dead or alive. Through all my pain blood sweat and tears you were there.

I owe you my life and that's no jive.

I'm proud to tell the world that's you are my mom. Without a doubt you are truly the meaning of love. I want you to know that you are more than my mother and friend, lovely lady; you are my everything…

You are My Strength:

Loving you is all I want to do

You are all I ever need

Even on my dying bed sick and my bones start

To bleed;

I will only call on you.

I have trust and faith in you

You are the one who can make my mind, heart

And spirit brand new,

Your miracles, love, mercy and blessings are

Truly incredible.

My life will not be complete until I'm with

You so please make me right

Sometimes I can see you looking down

At me protecting and guiding me through the

Night,

I want to be next to you please keep me in

Your light.

Knowing that you are here for me and you care about me is a beautiful blessing

I'm going to keep marching on through the

Storm because I know heaven is peaceful happy

Loving and warm, it's good to know when I'm

Weak I'm strong because God, you are my strength…

Victoria Nina Simone Robinson

A poem for you from Daddy

Tori I love you more than you will ever know

You have open my eyes up to what is real and important and changed me in so many ways all I do is for you all I have is yours I work hard so that you can have the best life possible the only thing I ask as your father is that you respect and appreciate the foundation I build for you.

Remember to always be a good young lady respect yourself as well as others be a role model in a positive way never let no man or woman take advantage of you and never let a man make you feel worthless because you are truly a beautiful child of God therefore you are priceless never sell your soul for money or material things because anything you need or want I will provide for you.

I want you to be educated and attend college and learn as many positive things you possibly can in life you will see as you get older just how important education is.

Never lie, cheat or steal to get what you want always be honest and work hard you will appreciate it more when you work for what you need and want.

I pray God blesses me to live a long life so that I can enjoy it with you and your mother my only goal is to make you a happy daughter and mommy a happy wife because I love you both more than words can express Victoria you are a blessing to the entire family you and your cousin Payton are our beautiful blessing and I want the best for you both it is important for you and your cousin to love respect and watch out for one another and never let each other do anything that will hurt you or your cousin have pride and dignity but be humble.

When you need help always come to me for assistance never try to handle everything on your own as your father I am supposed to help you and teach you about the world and people in it.

Understand that everyone is not going to be your friend or show love and kindness but know that you have a father, mother and family who loves you and will support you my beautiful daughter you are loved more than you know.

Always remember to pray and trust and God and ask him to direct you where you need to go in life I will always pray with you and for my child simply because I want the best for you.

I love you Tori always and forever

Simone:

My cousin and my sister you will always be I am very proud of the woman you have become you have achieved many of your goals and overcome lots of obstacles you are truly blessed and always have been a blessing to me.

You and I have had our share of ups and downs with one another but still the love remained and only grew to be stronger whenever you call on me I promise to be there no matter what the situation is trust and believe I will be there.

You are a great mother as well as a great person never let anyone steal your joy you deserve to be happy in every way, you are my heart and it's important to me that you smile every day.

Continue to pray and ask God to guide you in the way you should go because he knows best and God will care for you like no one can so as you journey through this life be blessed and move forward and conquer you dreams and goals.

Remember that your family loves you always and forever words of encouragement and love from your cousin/brother Pop.

Ps: I love you Monie bone lol

If there is anything that I would have to say to those who read my book I pray that you receive the most positive message from my words and it encourages you to change your ways and achieve your goals and definitely live a life that will allow you to be happy and successful and free of sin. I feel that if you focus on love, peace and respect a lot of the madness we have today would disappear so let's stop the hate and the violence and spread peace across the land.

I want to thank you for supporting my book I truly appreciate the support and love.

Sincerely Your Friend

Donald D Robinson II

Better known to many as POP/Pop the writer

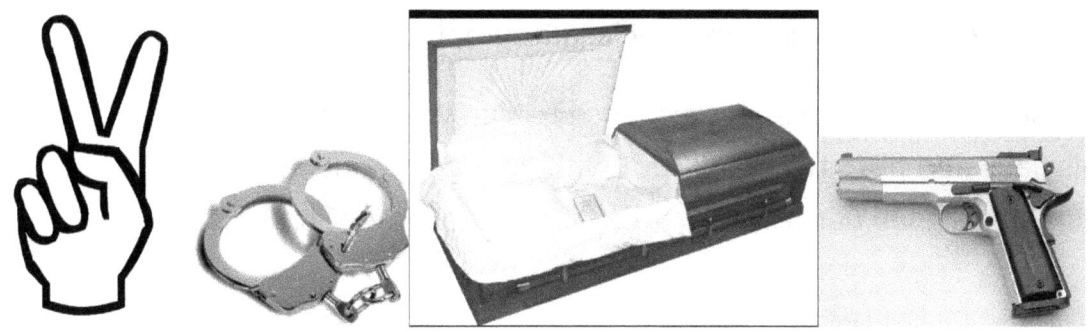

Which one will you choose A. Peace

B. The Handcuffs

C. The Coffin

D. The Gun

I pray and hope that you choose peace the most powerful weapon of all and also the key to having a happy life. There is nothing wrong with being peaceful and teaching others how to be peaceful.

This last page of my book is my special autograph page

For those who I may never get a chance to sign your book just flip to this page and fill in the blank spot with your name and you will also find my signed name with words of encouragement for you.

To:_____

May you enjoy reading my book and I hope that it helps you in every way possible I appreciate your support and I pray and ask God to keep you in good health help you to achieve your goals and mold you into the person you want and need to be. And remember not to walk around bitter and angry it will only cause you to become mentally and physically sick and lose the ones who care for you the most. Enjoy life but do it in a fun positive manner and always love yourself in the right way.

Sincerely yours

Donald David Robinson II